LITTLE TREE

E.E. CUMMINGS (1894–1962)

little tree
little silent Christmas tree
you are so little
you are more like a flower

who found you in the green forest
and were you very sorry to come away?
see   i will comfort you
because you smell so sweetly

i will kiss your cool bark
and hug you safe and tight
just as your mother would,
only don't be afraid

look   the spangles
that sleep all the year in a dark box
dreaming of being taken out and allowed to

                              shine,
the balls the chains red and gold the fluffy

                              threads,

put up your little arms
and i'll give them all to you to hold
every finger shall have its ring
and there won't be a single place dark or unhappy

then when you're quite dressed
you'll stand in the window for everyone to see
and how they'll stare!
oh but you'll be very proud

and my little sister and i will take hands
and looking up our beautiful tree
we'll dance and sing
"Noel Noel"

CHRISTMAS

GEORGE HERBERT (1593-1633)

I

After all pleasures as I rid one day,
My horse and I, both tired, body and mind,
With full cry of affections, quite astray;
I took up the next inn I could find.

There when I came, whom found I but my dear,
My dearest Lord, expecting till the grief
Of pleasures brought me to Him, ready there
To be all passengers' most sweet relief?

Oh Thou, whose glorious, yet contracted light,
Wrapt in night's mantle, stole into a manger;
Since my dark soul and brutish is Thy right,
To man of all beasts be not Thou a stranger:

Furnish and deck my soul, that Thou mayst have
A better lodging, than a rack, or grave.

The shepherds sing; and shall I silent be?
    My God, no hymn for Thee?
My soul's a shepherd too; a flock it feeds
    Of thoughts, and words, and deeds.
The pasture is Thy word: the streams, Thy grace
    Enriching all the place.
Shepherd and flock shall sing, and all my powers
    Outsing the daylight hours.
Then will we chide the sun for letting night
    Take up his place and right:
We sing one common Lord; wherefore he should
    Himself the candle hold.
I will go searching, till I find a sun
    Shall stay, till we have done;
A willing shiner, that shall shine as gladly,
    As frost-nipped suns look sadly.
Then will we sing, and shine all our own day,
    And one another pay:
His beams shall cheer my breast, and both so
                         twine,
Till ev'n His beams sing, and my music shine.

BURNING THE CHRISTMAS GREENS

WILLIAM CARLOS WILLIAMS (1883-1968)

Their time past, pulled down
cracked and flung to the fire
—go up in a roar

All recognition lost, burnt clean
clean in the flame, the green
dispersed, a living red,
flame red, red as blood wakes
on the ash—

and ebbs to a steady burning
the rekindled bed become
a landscape of flame

At the winter's midnight
we went to the trees, the coarse
holly, the balsam and
the hemlock for their green

At the thick of the dark
the moment of the cold's

deepest plunge we brought branches
cut from the green trees

to fill our need, and over
doorways, about paper Christmas
bells covered with tinfoil
and fastened by red ribbons

we stuck the green prongs
in the windows hung
woven wreaths and above pictures
the living green. On the

mantle we built a green forest
and among those hemlock
sprays put a herd of small
white deer as if they

were walking there. All this!
and it seemed gentle and good
to us. Their time past,
relief! The room bare. We

stuffed the dead grate
with them upon the half burnt out
log's smouldering eye, opening
red and closing under them

and we stood there looking down.
Green is a solace
a promise of peace, a fort
against the cold (though we

did not say so) a challenge
above the snow's
hard shell. Green (we might
have said) that, where

small birds hide and dodge
and lift their plaintive
rallying cries, blocks for them
and knocks down

the unseeing bullets of
the storm. Green spruce boughs
pulled down by a weight of
snow—Transformed!

Violence leaped and appeared.
Recreant! roared to life
as the flame rose through and
our eyes recoiled from it.

In the jagged flames green
to red, instant and alive. Green!
those sure abutments . . . Gone!
lost to mind

and quick in the contracting
tunnel of the grate
appeared a world! Black
mountains, black and red—as

yet uncolored—and ash white,
an infant landscape of shimmering
ash and flame and we, in
that instant, lost,

breathless to be witnesses,
as if we stood
ourselves refreshed among
the shining fauna of that fire.

VENI, VENI EMMANUEL

(TRADITIONAL, *circa* 850 A.D.)

O come, O come Emmanuel,
And ransom captive Israel,
That mourns in lonely exile here,
Until the Son of God appear.
Rejoice! Rejoice! Emmanuel
Shall come to thee O Israel.

O come, Thou Root of Jesse's tree,
An ensign of Thy people be;
Before Thee rulers silent fall;
All peoples on Thy mercy call.
Rejoice! Rejoice! Emmanuel
Shall come to thee O Israel.

O come, Thou Key of David, come,
And open wide our heavenly home;
Make safe the way that leads on high,
And close the path to misery.
Rejoice! Rejoice! Emmanuel
Shall come to thee O Israel.

O come, Desire of nations, bind
In one the hearts of all mankind;
Bid Thou our sad divisions cease,
And be Thyself our King of Peace.
Rejoice! Rejoice! Emmanuel
Shall come to thee O Israel.

Oh, come, strong branch of Jesse, free
Thine own from Satans tyranny;
From depths of hell Thy people save
And give them vict'ry o'er the grave.
Rejoice! Rejoice! Emmanuel
Shall come to thee O Israel.

Oh, come, oh, come, great Lord of might,
Who to Thy tribes on Sinai's height
In Ancient times once gave the law
In cloud, and majesty and awe.
Rejoice! Rejoice! Emmanuel
Shall come to thee O Israel.

English translation by John Neale, 1818–1866

IN THE BLEAK MID-WINTER

CHRISTINA ROSSETTI (1830-1894)

In the bleak mid-winter
    Frosty wind made moan,
Earth stood hard as iron,
    Water like a stone;
Snow had fallen, snow on snow,
    Snow on snow,
In the bleak mid-winter
    Long ago.

Our God, Heaven cannot hold Him
    Nor earth sustain;
Heaven and earth shall flee away
    When He comes to reign:
In the bleak mid-winter
    A stable-place sufficed
The Lord God Almighty,
    Jesus Christ.

Enough for Him, whom cherubim
    Worship night and day,
A breastful of milk

And a mangerful of hay;
Enough for Him, whom angels
    Fall down before,
The ox and ass and camel
    Which adore.

Angels and archangels
    May have gathered there,
Cherubim and seraphim
    Thronged the air,
But His mother only
    In her maiden bliss,
Worshipped the Beloved
    With a kiss.

What can I give Him,
    Poor as I am?
If I were a shepherd
    I would bring a lamb,
If I were a wise man
    I would do my part,
Yet what I can I give Him,
    Give my heart.

THE CHERRY TREE CAROL

(ANONYMOUS—FIFTEENTH CENTURY)

When Joseph was an old man, an old man was he,
He married Virgin Mary, The Queen of Galilee,
He married Virgin Mary, The Queen of Galilee.

When Joseph and Mary went walking one day
In a garden of cherries, they happened to stray,
In a garden of cherries, they happened to stray.

Then Mary spoke to Joseph, so meek and so mild,
"Joseph, gather me some cherries,

for I am with Child,
Joseph, gather me some cherries,

for I am with Child."

Then Joseph flew in anger, in anger flew he,
"Let the father of the baby gather cherries for thee,
Let the father of the baby gather cherries for thee."

Then Jesus spoke a few words from his mother's

womb,

"Bow low down, cherry tree,
                bow low down to the ground,
Bow low down, cherry tree,
                bow low down to the ground."

Then the cherry tree bowed low,
                bowed low down to the ground,
And Mary gathered cherries,
                while Joseph stood around,
And Mary gathered cherries,
                while Joseph stood around.

Then Joseph took Mary all on his right knee: crying
"Tell me, pretty baby, when thy birthday will be?
Tell me, pretty baby, when thy birthday will be?"

CHRISTMAS EAST OF THE BLUE RIDGE

CHARLES WRIGHT (b. 1935)

So autumn comes to an end with these few wet
                                        sad stains
Stuck to the landscape,
                    December dark
Running its hands through the lank hair of late
                                        afternoon,
Little tongues of the rain holding forth
                                under the eaves,
Such wash, such watery worlds. . . .

So autumn comes to this end,
And winter's vocabulary, downsized and
                                        distanced,
Drop by drop
Captures the conversation with its monosyllabic
                                        gutturals
And tin music,
            gravelly consonants, scratched vowels.

Soon the camel drivers will light their fires, soon
the stars
Will start on their brief dip down from the back
of heaven,
Down to the desert's dispensation
And night reaches, the gall and first birth,
The second only one word from now,
one word and its death from right now.

Meanwhile, in Charlottesville, the half moon
Hums like a Hottentot
high over Monticello
Clouds dishevel and rag out,
The alphabet of our discontent
Keeps on with its lettering,
gold on the black walls of our hearts. . . .

NATIVITY

JOHN DONNE (1572-1631)

Immensity cloistered in thy dear womb,
Now leaves His well-belov'd imprisonment,
There He hath made Himself to His intent
Weak enough, now into the world to come;
But O, for thee, for Him, hath the inn no room?
Yet lay Him in this stall, and from the Orient,
Stars and wise men will travel to prevent
The effect of Herod's jealous general doom.
Seest thou, my soul, with thy faith's eyes, how He
Which fills all place, yet none holds Him, doth lie?
Was not His pity towards thee wondrous high,
That would have need to be pitied by thee?
Kiss Him, and with Him into Egypt go,
With His kind mother, who partakes thy woe.

AS DEW IN APRIL

(ANONYMOUS—FIFTEENTH CENTURY)

I sing of a maiden
    That is makeless;
King of all kings
    To her son she ches.

He came all so still
    To his mother's bower,
As dew in April
    That falleth on the flower.

He came all so still
    There his mother lay,
As dew in April
    That falleth on the spray.

Mother and maiden
    Was never none but she;
Well may such a lady
    Goddes mother be.

(*"makeless"—matchless. "ches"—chose.*)

WINTER SCENE

A.R. AMMONS (1926-2001)

There is now not a single
leaf on the cherry tree:

except when the jay
plummets in, lights, and,

in pure clarity, squalls:
then every branch

quivers and
breaks out in blue leaves.

THE MAGI

WILLIAM BUTLER YEATS (1865-1939)

Now as at all times I can see in the mind's eye,
In their stiff, painted clothes, the pale unsatisfied ones
Appear and disappear in the blue depth of the sky
With all their ancient faces like rain-beaten stones,
And all their helms of silver hovering side by side,
And all their eyes still fixed, hoping to find once more,
Being by Calvary's turbulence unsatisfied,
The uncontrollable mystery on the bestial floor.

A SONG OF THE VIRGIN MOTHER

LOPE DE VEGA (1562-1635)

As ye go through these palm-trees
O holy angels;
Sith sleepeth my child here
Still ye the branches.

O Bethlehem palm-trees
That move to the anger
Of winds in their fury,
Tempestuous voices,
Make ye no clamor,
Run ye less swiftly,
Sith sleepeth the child here
Still ye your branches.

He the divine child
Is here a-wearied
Of weeping the earth-pain,
Here for his rest would he
Cease from his mourning,
Only a little while,

Sith sleepeth this child here
Stay ye the branches.

Cold be the fierce winds,
Treacherous round him.
Ye see that I have not
Wherewith to guard him,
O angels, divine ones
That pass us a-flying,
Sith sleepeth my child here
Stay ye the branches.

Translated from the Spanish by Ezra Pound

THE SAVIOR MUST HAVE BEEN A DOCILE GENTLEMAN

EMILY DICKINSON (1830-1886)

The Savior must have been
A docile Gentleman —
To come so far so cold a Day
For little Fellowmen —

The Road to Bethlehem
Since He and I were Boys
Was leveled, but for that 'twould be
A rugged Billion Miles —

TWAS JUST THIS TIME, LAST YEAR, I DIED

EMILY DICKINSON

Twas just this time, last year, I died.
I know I heard the Corn,
When I was carried by the Farms —
It had the Tassels on —

I thought how yellow it would look —
When Richard went to mill —
And then, I wanted to get out,
But something held my will.

I thought just how Red — Apples wedged
The Stubble's joints between —
And the Carts stooping round the fields
To take the Pumpkins in —

I wondered which would miss me, least,
And when Thanksgiving, came,
If Father'd multiply the plates —
To make an even Sum —

And would it blur the Christmas glee
My Stocking hang too high
For any Santa Claus to reach
The Altitude of me —

But this sort, grieved myself,
And so, I thought the other way,
How just this time, some perfect year —
Themself, should come to me —

KARMA

EDWIN ARLINGTON ROBINSON (1869-1935)

Christmas was in the air and all was well
With him, but for a few confusing flaws
In divers of God's images. Because
A friend of his would neither buy nor sell,
Was he to answer for the axe that fell?
He pondered; and the reason for it was,
Partly, a slowly freezing Santa Claus
Upon the corner, with his beard and bell.

Acknowledging an improvident surprise,
He magnified a fancy that he wished
The friend of whom he had wrecked were here
again.
Not sure of that, he found a compromise;
And from the fulness of his heart he fished
A dime for Jesus who had died for men.

FROM **ON THE MORNING OF CHRIST'S NATIVITY**

JOHN MILTON (1608-1674)

I

This is the month, and this the happy morn,
Wherein the Son of Heaven's eternal King,
Of wedded maid and virgin mother born,
Our great redemption from above did bring;
For so the holy sages once did sing,
   That He our deadly forfeit should release,
And with His Father work us a perpetual peace.

II

That glorious Form, that Light unsufferable,
And that far-beaming blaze of Majesty,
Wherewith He wont at Heaven's high council-table
To sit the midst of Trinal Unity,
He laid aside; and here with us to be
 Forsook the courts of everlasting day,
And chose with us a darksome house of mortal clay.

III

Say Heavenly Muse, shall not thy sacred vein
Afford a present to the Infant God?
Hast thou no verse, no hymn, or solemn strain,
To welcome Him to this His new abode,
Now while the Heaven, by the Sun's team untrod,
    Hath took no print of the approaching light,
And all the spangled host keep watch in squadrons
                              bright?

IV

See how from far upon the eastern road
The star-led wizards haste with odours sweet!
O run, prevent them with thy humble ode,
And lay it lowly at His blessed feet;
Have thou the honour first thy Lord to greet,
    And join thy voice unto the angel quire,
From out His secret altar touched with hallowed
                              fire.

DUST OF SNOW

ROBERT FROST

The way a crow
Shook down on me
The dust of snow
From a hemlock tree

Has given my heart
A change of mood
And saved some part
Of a day I had rued.

from **RORATE CELI DESUPER**

WILLIAM DUNBAR (c.1460 -c.1515)

Rorate celi desuper![1]
Ye Heavens distil your balmy shouris
For now is risen the bright day star
Fae the rose Mary, flour of flouris;
The clear Son, whom no cloud devouris,
Surmounting Phoebus in the east,
Is comen of his heavenly touris;
Et nobis Puer natus est[2]

Celestial fowlis in the air
Sing wi' your notis upon hight
In flrthis and in Forestis fair
Be mirthful now, at all your might
For passit is your dully night;
Aurora has the cloudis pierc'd,
The sun is risen with gladsome light,
Et nobis Puer natus est

Sing heaven imperial, most of hight
Regions of air mak harmony;
A' fish in flood and fowl of flight
Be mirthful and mak melody:
All Gloria In Excelsis cry,
Heaven, erd, sea, man, bird, and beast,
He that is crownit abune the sky
Pro nobis Puer natus est[3]

(1. *Drop down ye heavens from above.* 2&3. *Unto us a son is born.*
"shouris"—showers. "Fae"—From. "flour"—flower. "touris"—tow-
ers. "firthis"—firths. "A'"—all. "erd"—earth. "abune"—above.)

COME, BRING WITH A NOISE

ROBERT HERRICK (1591–1674)

Come, bring with a noise,
　My merrie merrie boys,
The Christmas Log to the firing;
　While my good dame, she
　Bids ye all be free,
And drink to your hearts' desiring.

With the last year's brand
　Light the new block, and,
For good success in his spending,
　On your psalt'ries play,
　That sweet luck may
Come while the Log is attending.

Drink now the strong beer,
　Cut the white loaf here,
The while the meat is a shredding;
　For the rare Mince pie
　And the plums stand by
To fill the paste that's a kneading.

WHAT SWEETER MUSIC CAN WE BRING

ROBERT HERRICK

What sweeter music can we bring
Than a carol for to sing
The birth of this our heavenly king
Awake the voice! Awake the string
Dark and dull night fly hence away,
And give the honor of this day
That sees December turned to May.

If we may ask the reason, say
The why and wherefore all things here
Seem like the Springtime of the year
Why does the chilling Winter's morn
Smile like a field beset with corn
We see him come and know him ours,
Who with his sunshine and his showers
Turns all the patient ground to flowers.

The Darling of the world is come
And fit it is we find a room
To welcome Him, the nobler part
Of all this house here is the heart
Which we will give Him and bequeath
This holly and this ivy wreath
To do Him honour who's our King
And Lord of all this revelling.

BERNADETTE MAYER (b. 1945)

Come now
It's Midwinter Day today a day
To cause the sun to stand still as it will anyway
At a point on its ecliptic furthest away
And from now on, they say, things will turn our
                                                                        way
To me the sun complains of such a phony
                                                          culmination
The Great mistaken Circle of the Celestial
                                                          Sphere,
Sun's apparent annual path, man's mere erudition,
Old egocentric notions of who is who and what is
                                                                      where
                          Here
Winter makes us wet and cold and old
Like a man of eighty winters who will keep
Hot food on the rickety stove like stories told
To pass midwinter night and never sleep
                          It's December
It's the dead of winter, remember

Sun setting red on the hill of red trees
Cold dusk's blue clouds white skies
I count the days

            I dream

A VISIT FROM ST. NICHOLAS

CLEMENT CLARK MOORE (1779-1863)

'Twas the night before Christmas, when all
                         through the house
Not a creature was stirring, not even a mouse;
The stockings were hung by the chimney with care,
In hopes that St. Nicholas soon would be there;
The children were nestled all snug in their beds,
While visions of sugar-plums danced in their heads;
And mamma in her 'kerchief, and I in my cap,
Had just settled our brains for a long winter's nap,
When out on the lawn there arose such a clatter,
I sprang from the bed to see what was the matter.
Away to the window I flew like a flash,
Tore open the shutters and threw up the sash.
The moon on the breast of the new-fallen snow
Gave the lustre of mid-day to objects below,
When, what to my wondering eyes should appear,
But a miniature sleigh, and eight tiny reindeer,
With a little old driver, so lively and quick,
I knew in a moment it must be St. Nick.
More rapid than eagles his coursers they came,

And he whistled, and shouted, and called them by
name;
"Now, Dasher! now, Dancer! now, Prancer and
Vixen!
On, Comet! on, Cupid! on, Donner and Blitzen!
To the top of the porch! to the top of the wall!
Now dash away! dash away! dash away all!"
As dry leaves that before the wild hurricane fly,
When they meet with an obstacle, mount to the sky;
So up to the house-top the coursers they flew,
With the sleigh full of Toys, and St. Nicholas too.
And then, in a twinkling, I heard on the roof
The prancing and pawing of each little hoof.
As I drew in my head, and was turning around,
Down the chimney St. Nicholas came with a bound.
He was dressed all in fur, from his head to his foot,
And his clothes were all tarnished with ashes and
soot;
A bundle of Toys he had flung on his back,
And he looked like a pedler just opening his pack.
His eyes—how they twinkled! his dimples how
merry!
His cheeks were like roses, his nose like a cherry!
His droll little mouth was drawn up like a bow

And the beard of his chin was as white as the snow;
The stump of a pipe he held tight in his teeth,
And the smoke it encircled his head like a wreath;
He had a broad face and a little round belly,
That shook when he laughed, like a bowlful of jelly.
He was chubby and plump, a right jolly old elf,
And I laughed when I saw him, in spite of myself;
A wink of his eye and a twist of his head,
Soon gave me to know I had nothing to dread;
He spoke not a word, but went straight to his work,
And filled all the stockings; then turned with a jerk,
And laying his finger aside of his nose,
And giving a nod, up the chimney he rose;
He sprang to his sleigh, to his team gave a whistle,
And away they all flew like the down of a thistle,
But I heard him exclaim, ere he drove out of sight,
"Happy Christmas to all, and to all a good-night."

A CHRISTMAS CARD

THOMAS MERTON (1915-1968)

When the white stars talk together like sisters
And when the winter hills
Raise their grand semblance in the freezing night,
Somewhere one window
Bleeds like the brown eye of an open forge.

Hills, stars,
White stars that stand above the eastern stable,
Look down and offer Him
The dim adoring light of your belief
Whose small Heart bleeds with infinite fire.

Shall not this Child
(When we shall hear the bells of His amazing
                                                    voice)
Conquer the winter of our hateful century?

And when his Lady Mother leans upon the crib,
Lo, with what rapiers
Those two loves fence and flame their brilliancy!

Here in this straw lie planned the fires
That will melt all our sufferings:
He is our Lamb, our holocaust!

And one by one the shepherds, with their snowy feet,
Stamp and shake out their hats upon the stable dirt,
And one by one kneel down to look upon their Life.

CHRISTMAS CARD TO GRACE HARTIGAN

FRANK O'HARA (1926-1966)

There's no holly, but there is
the glass and granite towers
and the white stone lions
and the pale violet clouds. And
the great tree of balls in
Rockefeller Plaza is public.

Christmas is green and general
like all great works of the
imagination, swelling from minute
private sentiments in the desert,
a wreath around our intimacy
like children's voices in a park.

For red there is our blood
which, like your smile, must be
protected from spilling into
generality by secret meanings,
the lipstick of life hidden
in a handbag against violations.

Christmas is the time of cold air
and loud parties and big expense,
but in our hearts flames flicker
answeringly, as on old-fashioned
trees. I would rather the house
burn down than our flames go out.

FROM **THE SECOND NUN'S TALE**

CHAUCER (1340-1400)

Thou mayde and mooder, doghter of thy sone,
Thou welle of mercy, sinful soules cure,
In whom that god, for bountee, chees to wone,
Thou humble, and heigh over every creature,
Thou nobledest so ferforth our nature.
That no desdeyn the maker hadde of kinde,
His sone in blode and flesh to clothe and winde.

Withinne the cloistre blisful of thy sydes
Took mannes shap the eternal love and pees,
That of the tryne compas lord and gyde is,
Whom erthe and see and heven, out of relees,
Ay herien: and thou, virgin wemmelees,
Bar of thy body, and dweltest mayden pure,
The creatour of every creature.

Assembled is in thee magnificence
With mercy, goodnesse, and with swich pitee
That thou, that art the sonne of excellence,
Nat only helpest hem that preyen thee,

But ofte tyme, of thy benignitee,
Ful frely, er that men thyn help biseche,
Thou goost biforn, and art hir lyves leche.

("wone"—dwell. "ferforth"—far. "tryne compas" '—threefold world.
"out of relees"—without ceasing. "Ay herein"— ever praise. "wem-
melees"— stainless. "leche"— physician.)

Chaucer was thoroughly familiar with the works of Dante and
often paraphrased him in his own poety. Here are the sixth,
seventh, and eighth stanzas of Chaucer's *Second Nun's Tale*

THE OXEN

THOMAS HARDY (1840-1928)

Christmas Eve, and twelve of the clock.
"Now they are all on their knees,"
An elder said as we sat in a flock
By the embers in hearthside ease.

We pictured the meek mild creatures where
They dwelt in their strawy pen,
Nor did it occur to one of us there
To doubt they were kneeling then.

So fair a fancy few would weave
In these years! Yet, I feel,
If someone said on Christmas Eve,
"Come; see the oxen kneel

"In the lonely barton by yonder coomb
Our childhood used to know,"
I should go with him in the gloom,
Hoping it might be so.

THE CARRIER OF THE MASSACHUSETTS *SPY* WISHES ALL HIS CUSTOMERS A MERRY CHRISTMAS AND A HAPPY NEW YEAR AND PRESENTS THE FOLLOWING, VIZ.

Hail happy day, important year!
Be more propitious than the last;
In thee let mighty TRUTH appear,
And every fool and tyrant blast.

From this UNBOUGHT, UNFETTERED PRESS,
Which laws and constitutions show;
That it the happy land may bless,
With lessons which they ought to know.

Nor shall the frowns of Low'ring skies,
Nor party rage of selfish men,
Forbid the boy who brings your SPYS,
To serve and pleasure you again.

But Sirs, since your indulgent hands
Are yearly wont my heart to chear;
Some pence will rivet your commands, and
And fix my wishes for the year

Boston, Jan. 1, 1772

I HEARD THE BELLS
ON CHRISTMAS DAY

HENRY WADSWORTH LONGFELLOW (1807-1882)

I heard the bells on Christmas day
Their old familiar carols play,
 And wild and sweet
 The words repeat
Of peace on earth, good will to men.

I thought how, as the day had come,
The belfries of all Christendom
 Had rolled along
 Th' unbroken song
Of peace on earth, good will to men.

Then from each black, accurséd mouth
The cannon thundered in the South,
 And with the sound
 The carols drowned
Of peace on earth, good will to men.

It was as if an earthquake rent
The hearth-stones of a continent,

And made forlorn
The households born
Of peace on earth, good will to men.

And in despair I bowed my head
"There is no peace on earth," I said,
"For hate is strong
And mocks the song
Of peace on earth, good will to men."

Then pealed the bells more loud and deep:
"God is not dead, nor doth He sleep;
The wrong shall fail,
The right prevail
With peace on earth, good will to men."

Till ringing, swinging on its way,
The world revolved from night to day,
A voice, a chime,
A chant sublime,
Of peace on earth, good will to men

Still despondent from the death of his wife from a fire in 1861,
Longfellow wrote this poem on Christmas Day 1864 after he
received news that his son Charles Appleton Longfellow had
been wounded in a battle of the Civil War.

XMAS

ROBERT CREELEY (1926-2005)

I'm sure there's a world I
can get to by walking another
block in the direction that
was pointed out to me by any-

one I was with and would even
talk to me that late at
night and with everything
confused—I know—the

kids tired, nerves stretched—
and all, and this person, old
man, Santa Claus! by
god—the reindeer, the presents.

FROM **THE FOURTH ECLOGUE**

VIRGIL (70 B.C.-19 B.C.)

Muses
Muses of Sicily
Now let us sing a serious song
There are taller trees than the apple and the
                                    crouching tamerisk
If we sing of the woods, let our forest be stately

Now the last age is coming
As it was written in the Sybil's book
The great circle of the centuries begins again
Justice, the Virgin, has returned to earth
With all of Saturn's court
A new line is sent down to us from the skies
And thou, Lucina, must smile
Smile for the birth of the boy, the blessed boy
For whom they will beat their swords into
                                    ploughshares
For whom the golden race will rise, the whole
                                    world new
Smile, pure Lucina, smile
Thine own Apollo will reign

And thou, Pollio
It is in thy term this glorious age begins
And the great months begin their march
When we shall lose all trace of the old guilt
And the world learn to forget fear
For the boy will become divine
He will see gods and heroes
And will himself be seen by them as god and hero
As he rules over a world of peace
A world made peaceful by his father's wisdom

For thee, little boy, will the earth pour forth gifts
All untilled, give thee gifts
First the wandering ivy and foxglove
Then colocasia and the laughing acanthus
Uncalled the goats will come home with their milk
No longer need the herds fear the lion
Thy cradle itself will bloom with sweet flowers
The serpent will die
The poison plant will wither
Assyrian herbs will spring up everywhere

But when thou hast grown strong and become a man
Then even the trader will leave the sea
His pine ship carry no more wares
And everywhere the land will yield all things that
                                        life requires
No longer need the ground endure the harrow
Nor the vine the pruning hook
The farmer can free his oxen from the yoke
Then colored cloths no longer will need lying dyes
For the ram in the field will change his own fleece
To soft purple or saffron yellow
Each grazing lamb will have a scarlet coat

"Onward, O glorious ages, onward"
Thus sang the fatal sisters to their spindles
Chanting together the unalterable Will

Go forward, little boy, to thy great honors
Soon comes thy time
Dear child of gods from whom a Jupiter will come
See how for thee the world nods its huge head
All lands and seas and endless depths of sky
See how the earth rejoices in the age that is to be

Learn, little boy, to greet thy mother with a smile

For thee she has endured nine heavy months

Learn, little boy, to smile

For if thou didst not smile

And if thy parents did not smile on thee

No god could ask thee to his table

No goddess to her bed.

Surely Virgil's "prophetic" Eclogue must be the oldest of all
Christmas poems, for it was written about 40 B.C. Actually
the poet sang of the coming Golden Age to honor the birth of
the son of Pollio, an important Roman politician of the day.
But the people of the Middle Ages became convinced that
Virgil had had a revelation and was really announcing the
birth of the King of Kings. It was the Emperor Constantine
himself who first publicized the idea. Later the allegory was
developed by the learned scholar Servius and by many others
after him. Thus Virgil came to be almost a saint in the minds
of Christian writers, and Dante chose him for his guide on the
path of salvation in the *Divine Comedy*. This translation is by
James Laughlin.

CHRISTMAS

STEVIE SMITH (1903-1971)

A child is born, they cry, a child
And he is Noble and not Mild
(It is the child that makes them wild)

The King sits brooding on his throne
He looks around and calls a man:
My men bring me a heavy stone.

My men bring me a purple robe
And bring me whips and iron goad.
They brought them to him where he strode.

My men bring gold and bring incense
And fetch all noble children at once
That I shall never take offence.

The men fetched the noble children away
They lifted them up and cried: Hurray.
The King sat back and clapped their play.

All noble mild children are brought home
To the wicked King who has cast them down
And ground their bones on the heavy stone.

But the child that is Noble and not Mild
He lies in his cot. He is unbeguiled.
He is Noble, he is not Mild,
And he is born to make men wild.

CHRISTMAS CAROL

PAUL LAWRENCE DUNBAR (1872-1906)

Ring out, ye bells!
All Nature swells
With gladness at the wondrous story—
The world was lorn,
But Christ is born
To change our sadness into glory.

Sing, earthlings, sing!
To-night a King
Hath come from heaven's high throne to bless us.
The outstretched hand
O'er all the land
Is raised in pity to caress us.

Come at his call;
Be joyful all;
Away with mourning and with sadness!
The heavenly choir
With holy fire
Their voices raise in songs of gladness.

The darkness breaks
And Dawn awakes,
Her cheeks suffused with youthful blushes.
The rocks and stones
In holy tones
Are singing sweeter than the thrushes.

Then why should we
In silence be,
When Nature lends her voice to praises;
When heaven and earth
Proclaim the truth
Of Him for whom that lone star blazes?

No, be not still,
But with a will
Strike all your harps and set them ringing;
On hill and heath
Let every breath
Throw all its power into singing!

CHRIST CLIMBED DOWN

LAWRENCE FERLINGHETTI (b. 1919)

Christ climbed down
from His bare tree
this year
and ran away to where
there were no rootless Christmas trees
hung with candycanes and breakable stars.

Christ climbed down
from His bare Tree
this year
and ran away to where
there were no gilded Christmas trees
and no tinsel Christmas trees
and no tinfoil Christmas trees
and no pink plastic Christmas trees
and no gold Christmas trees
and no black Christmas trees
and no powderblue Christmas trees
hung with electric candles
and encircled by tin electric trains
and clever cornball relatives.

Christ climbed down
from His bare Tree
this year
and ran away to where
no intrepid Bible salesmen
covered the territory
in two-tone cadillacs
and where no Sears Roebuck crèches
complete with plastic babe in manger
arrived by parcel post,
the babe by special delivery
and where no televised Wise Men
praised the Lord Calvert Whiskey

Christ climbed down
from His bare Tree
this year
and ran away to where
no fat handshaking stranger
in a red flannel suit
and a fake white beard
went around passing himself off
as some sort of North Pole saint

crossing the desert to Bethlehem
Pennsylvania
in a Volkswagen sled
drawn by rollicking Adirondack reindeer
with German names
and bearing sacks of Humble Gifts
from Saks Fifth Avenue
for everybody's imagined Christ child

Christ climbed down
from His bare Tree
this year
and ran away to where
no Bing Crosby carolers
groaned of a tight Christmas
and where no Radio City angels
iceskated wingless
thru a winter wonderland
into a jinglebell heaven
daily at 8:30
with Midnight Mass matinees

Christ climbed down
from his bare Tree

this year
and softly stole away into
some anonymous Mary's womb again
where in the darkest night
of everybody's anonymous soul
He awaits again
an unimaginable
and impossibly
Immaculate Reconception
the very craziest
of Second Comings.

FROM AS YOU LIKE IT
Act 2, Scene VII

WILLIAM SHAKESPEARE (1564-1616)

Blow, blow, thou winter wind,
Thou art not so unkind
As man's ingratitude;
Thy tooth is not so keen,
Because thou art not seen,
Although thy breath be rude.
Heigh ho, sing heigh ho, unto the green holly;
most friendship is feigning, most loving mere folly:
Then, heigh ho, the holly!
This life is most jolly.

Freeze, freeze, thou bitter sky,
That dost not bite so nigh
As benefits forgot:
Though thou the waters warp,
Thy sting is not so sharp
As friend remember'd not.
Heigh ho, sing heigh ho, unto the green holly:
most friendship is feigning, most loving mere folly:
Then, heigh ho, the holly!
This life is most jolly.

A CHRISTMAS GREETING

WALT WHITMAN (1819-1892)

Welcome, Brazilian brother—thy ample place is
                        ready;
A loving hand—a smile from the north—a sunny
                        instant hall!
(Let the future care for itself, where it reveals its
                        troubles, impedimentas,
Ours, our the present throe, the democratic aim,
                    the acceptance and the faith;)
To thee today our reaching arm, our turning
                        neck—to thee from us
the expectant eye,
Thou cluster free! thou brilliant lustrous one!
                        thou, learning well,
The true lesson of a nation's light in the sky,
(More shining than the Cross, more than the
                        Crown,)
The height to be superb humanity.

MINSTRALS

WILLIAM WORDSWORTH (1770-1850)

The minstrels played their Christmas tune
To-night beneath my cottage-eaves;
While, smitten by a lofty moon,
The encircling laurels, thick with leaves,
Gave back a rich and dazzling sheen,
That overpowered their natural green.

Through hill and valley every breeze
Had sunk to rest with folded wings:
Keen was the air, but could not freeze,
Nor check, the music of the strings;
So stout and hardy were the band
That scraped the chords with strenuous hand.

And who but listened?—till was paid
Respect to every inmate's claim,
The greeting given, the music played
In honour of each household name,
Duly pronounced with lusty call,
And "Merry Christmas" wished to all.

'THE HOLY ONE, BLESSED BE HE, WANDERS AGAIN,' SAID JACOB, 'HE IS WANDERING AND LOOKS FOR A PLACE WHERE HE CAN REST.'

DENISE LEVERTOV (1923-1997)

Between the pages
a wren's feather
to mark what passage?
Blood, not dry,
beaded scarlet on dusty stones.
A look of wonder
barely perceived on a turning face—
what, who had they seen?
Traces.
Here's the cold inn,
the wanderer passed it by
searching once more
for a stable's warmth,
a birthplace.

ST. BERNARD'S HYMN TO THE VIRGIN

DANTE (1265-1321)

Vergine Madre, figlia del tuo Figilo,
   Umile e alta più che creatura,
   Termine fisso d'etterno consiglio,

Tu se' colei che l'umana natura
   Nobilitasti sÌ che il suo Fattore
   Non disdegnÚ di farsi sua fattura.

Nel ventre tuo si raccese l'amore
   Per lo cui caldo me l'etterna pace
   Così è germinato questo fiore.

Qui sei a noi meridiana face
   Di caritate, e giuso intra i mortali
   Se' di speranza fontana vivace.

Donna, se' tanto grande e tanto vali
   Che qual vuol grazia ed a te non ricorre,
   Sua disianza vuol volar sanz' ali,

La tua benignità non pur soccorre
   A chi domanda, ma molte fiate
   Liberamente al dimandar precorre.

In te misericordia, in te pietate,
   in te magnificeuza, in te s'aduna
   Quantunque in creatura è di bontate.

Of the countless poems written in praise of the Virgin by far
the most wonderful is that which Dante puts in the mouth of
St. Bernard in the final canto of the *Divine Comedy*. No transla-
tion could possibly do justice to its perfection, so we give the
original Italian, followed by a rough prose paraphrase:

Virgin Mother, daughter of thine own Son, so humble yet more
exalted than any creature, fixed goal of the eternal plan, thou
art she who did so raise our human nature that its own Creator
was not ashamed to take its form, in thee was born the love
whose warmth has grown this flower in the timeless peace.
In heaven thou art the noonday torch of charity and below on
mortal earth thou art the living fountain of hope. Lady, thou
art so great and such is thy power that he who seeks grace and
does not turn for it to thee leaves his desire trying to fly without
wings. Such is thy kindness that it helps not only those who ask
but often freely goes before and helps before the asking. In thee
mercy, pity, magnificence and whatever goodness exists in any
creature are joined together.

THE SNOW MAN

WALLACE STEVENS (1879-1955)

One must have a mind of winter
To regard the frost and the boughs
Of the pine-trees crusted with snow;

And have been cold a long time
To behold the junipers shagged with ice,
The spruces rough in the distant glitter

Of the January sun; and not to think
Of any misery in the sound of the wind,
In the sound of a few leaves,

Which is the sound of the land
Full of the same wind
That is blowing in the same bare place

For the listener, who listens in the snow,
And, nothing himself, beholds
Nothing that is not there and the nothing that is.

THE BOAR'S HEAD CAROL

(TRADITIONAL–FIRST PUBLISHED 1521 BY
WYNKEN DE WORDE IN *CHRISTMASSE CAROLLES*)

The boar's head in hand bear I,
Bedeck'd with bays and rosemary.
I pray you, my masters, be merry
   Quot estis in convivio[1]

Caput apri defero
Reddens laudes Domino[2]

The boar's head, as I understand,
Is the rarest dish in all the land,
Which thus bedeck'd with a gay garland
   Let us servire cantico[3]

Caput apri defero
Reddens laudes Domino

Our steward hath provided this
In honor of the King of Bliss;
Which, on this day to be served is
   In Reginensi atrio.[4]

Caput apri defero

Reddens laudes Domino

(**1.** *As you all feast so heartily.* **2.** *Lo, behold the head I bring/*
Giving praise to God we sing. **3.** *Let us serve with a song.* **4.** *In the*
Queen's hall.)

GIGUE FOR CHRISTMAS EVE

MARIE PONSOT (b. 1921)

"O woman, go gently; the beast is too old
To get up a trot when his belly is cold
—Poor creature; your own, if the truth must be told
Is as tight as a drum and how long can it hold?"

"I forgot him, good Joseph, forgive me, now do.
Go easy, poor donkey; I forgot about you
With my thinking we'd soon get some village in
                                                view.
Do you take your own time, now, the night is still
                                                new."

"Man dear are you mad?" the beast whispered
                                                aside.
"Far worse heels than hers have belabored my side!
Why, the woman you mention is God's own good
                                                bride
And I'm honored to have her along for the ride."

"Don't I know it," said Joseph. "But don't let her

                             hear.

I say, 'Pity the donkey,' to capture her ear.

For herself she won't spare, and it's that that I fear

With the jog in this road that might bring her

                             down here."

"O good Joseph! No wonder God made you her man!

Your respect for her nature's a pleasure to scan.

Now if God speed me easy, I'll run the whole span

And get you to Bedlam, according to plan!"

Well, the donkey's brave words woke twelve

                             angels at least;

Four and twenty wings feathered the speed of the

                             beast,

Till in Bedlam his burden was gently released

Just in time for the star that roared out of the east.

JOSEPH'S SUSPICION

RAINER MARIA RILKE (1875-1926)

And the angel, taking some pains, told
Considerately the man who clenched his fists;
"But can't you see in her robe's every fold
That she is cool as the Lord's morning mists?"

But the other murmured, looking sinister:
"What is it that has wrought this change in her?"
Then cried the angel to him: "Carpenter,
Can't you see yet that God is acting here?"

"Because you plane the planks, of your pride could
You really make the Lord God answerable,
Who unpretentiously from the same wood
Makes the leaves burst forth, the young buds
                                  swell?"

He understood that. And then as he raised
His frightened glance toward the angel who
Had gone away . . . slowly the man drew
Off his heavy cap. Then in song he praised.

Translated from the German by C. F. MacIntyre

CHRISTMAS LETTER 1944

ROBERT DUNCAN (1919-1988)

Dear Mother, this by way of poem is little
more than Christmas greeting, by way of letter
sums more than a year, in and out, older
than not so long ago, but short
of the full greeting heart
might give had time not tamperd.

The face (looking up into the camera face)
fixes itself with as much grace
as it has in it. Lighted by clear air,
by reflected clean-washt rocks & shirt, the hair
shows blond. That was a good time of year
and place for a photograph
to catch so little wrath or fretful loving
showing in that face.

Christmas greeting would be care-free but's
                              modified
by such a worrying face by care, dyed
a deeper, coarser, relentless, red and green
in the heart's careful remorseful stain,

catching into itself, with more distortion
than camera caught this face, a portion
of Christ's love, more than Christmas evening
revelry. Christ's serious accusing love
that measures us short in what we bring
each to all the others is a cross of
judgment that marks each face
seeking grace.

This by way of Christmas greeting is little
less than poetry; by way of total
(the face, the photograph) is fair
I hope. Showing more of what is there
than others. It allows
a certain warmth to show, a pause,
A Christmas hiatus in the midst of battle.

The full greeting heart might give
is tamperd by each day we live.
In memory of Christ's love we live
each day untamperd by our life.
And in our narrow hearts Christ's gift
gives love's face toward the total life.

THE OLD YEAR NOW AWAY HAS FLED

TRADITIONAL (*circa.* 1642)

The old year now away is fled,
The new year it is entered;
Then let us now our sins down tread,
And joyfully all appear.
Let's merry be this day,
And let us now both sport and play
Hang grief! Cast care away —
God send you a happy new year!

And now with new-year gifts each friend
Unto each other they do send;
God grant we may all our lives amend,
And that the truth may appear.
Now, like the snake his skin,
Cast off all evil thoughts and sin,
And so the year begins —
God send us a happy new year!

AULD LANG SYNE

ROBERT BURNS (1759-1796)

Should auld acquaintance be forgot
And never brought to mind?
Should auld acquaintance be forgot,
And auld lang syne!

CHORUS

For auld lang syne, my jo,
For auld lang syne,
We'll tak a cup o' kindness yet,
For auld lang syne.

We twa hae run about the braes,
And pou'd the gowans fine;
But we've wander'd mony a weary fit,
Sin' auld lang syne.

CHORUS

We twa hae paidl'd in the burn,
Frae morning sun till dine;
But seas between us braid hae roar'd,
Sin' auld lang syne.

And surely ye'll be your pint-stowp
And surely I'll be mine
And we'll tak a cup o'kindness yet,
For auld lang syne.

And there's a hand, my trusty fiere!
And gie's a hand o' thine!
And we'll tak a right gude-willie-waught,
For auld lang syne.

Should auld acquaintance be forgot
And never brought to mind?
Should auld acquaintance be forgot,
And auld lang syne!

*("auld lang syne"—old long since/times gone by. "my jo"—my dear.
"gowans"—daisies. "fit"—foot. "braid"—broad. "fiere"—friend.
"gie's"— give us. "stowp"—tankard. "gude-willie-waught"—[good]
cordial drink together.)*

THE TRUE CHRISTMAS

HENRY VAUGHN (1621-1695)

So stick up *Ivie* and the *Bays*,
And then restore the *Heathen* ways.
Green will remind you of the spring,
Though this great day denies the thing.
And mortifies the earth and all
But your wild *Revels*, and loose *Hall*.
Could you wear *Flow'rs*, and *Roses* strow
Blushing upon your breasts' *warm Snow*,
That very *dress* your lightness will
Rebuke, and wither at the Ill.
The brightness of this day we owe
Not unto *Music*, *Masque*, nor *Show*:
Nor gallant *furniture*, nor *plate*;
But to the *Manger's* mean estate.
His *life* while here, as well as *birth*,
Was but a check to *pomp* and *mirth*;
And all man's *greatness* you may see
Condemned by His *humility*.

　　Then leave your open *house* and *noise*,
To welcome Him with *holy Joys*,
And the poor *Shepherd's* watchfulness:

Whom *light* and *hymns* from heaven did bless.

What you *abound* with, cast abroad

To those that *want*, and ease your load.

Who empties thus, will bring more in;

But riot is both *loss* and *Sin*.

Dress finely what comes not in sight,

And then you keep your *Christmas* right.

RED HOOK: DECEMBER

GEORGE OPPEN (1908-1984)

We had not expected it, the whole street
Lit with the red blue, green
And yellow of the Christmas lights
In the windows shining and blinking
Into distance down the cross streets.
The children are almost awed in the street
Putting out the trash paper
In the winking light. A man works
Patiently in his overcoat
With the little bulbs
Because the window is open
In December. The bells ring,

Ring electronically the New Year
Among the roofs
And one can be at peace
In this city on a shore
For the moment now
With wealth, the shining wealth.

I HAVE LIGHTED THE CANDLES, MARY

KENNETH PATCHEN (1911-1972)

I have lighted the candles, Mary.
How softly breathes your little Son

My wife has spread the table
With our best cloth. There are apples,
Bright as red clocks, upon the mantel.
The snow is a weary face at the window.
How sweetly does He sleep

"Into this bitter world, O Terrible Huntsman!"
I say, and she takes my hand—"Hush,
You will wake Him."

The taste of tears is on her mouth
When I kiss her. I take an apple
And hold it tightly in my fist;
The cold, swollen face of war leans in the

window.

They are blowing out the candles, Mary . . .
The world is a thing gone mad tonight.
O hold Him tenderly, dear Mother,
For He is a kingdom in the hearts of men.

Acknowledgments

Thanks are due to the following copyright holders for their permission to reprint the following poems: A.R. AMMONS: "Winter Scene" from *The Collected Poems of A.R. Ammons, 1951-1971*, © 1965 by A.R. Ammons. Reprinted by permission of W.W. Norton & Company, Inc. ROBERT CREELEY: "Xmas" from *Windows*, copyright ©1990 by by the University of California Press. Reprinted by permission of The University of California Press. E.E. CUMMINGS: "little tree" copyright 1920 by E.E. Cummings, originally printed in *Dial Magazine*. ROBERT DUNCAN: "Christmas Letter 1944" from *The Years as Catches* (Oyez: Berkeley, 1966), ©1966 by Robert Duncan. Used by permission from The Jess Collins Trust. LAWRENCE FERLINGHETTI: "Christ Climbed Down" from *A Coney Island of the Mind*, copyright ©1958 by Lawrence Ferlinghetti. Reprinted by permission of New Directions Publishing Corp. ROBERT FROST: "Dust of Snow" from *The Poetry Of Robert Frost* edited by Edward Connery Lathem. Copyright 1923, 1969 by Henry Holt and Company. Copyright 1951 by Robert Frost. Reprinted by permission of Henry Holt and Company, LLC. DENISE LEVERTOV: "The Holy One, Blessed Be He, Wanders Again" from *The Stream And The Sapphire*, copyright ©1997 by Denise Levertov. Reprinted by permission of New Directions Publishing Corp. BERNADETTE MAYER: "Midwinter Day" from *Midwinter Day*, copyright ©1982 by Bernadette Mayer. Reprinted by permission of New Directions Publishing Corp. THOMAS MERTON: "A Christmas Card" from *The Collected Poems Of Thomas Merton*, copyright ©1948 by New Directions Publishing Corporation. Reprinted by permission of New Directions Publishing Corp. FRANK O'HARA: "A Christmas Card to Grace Hartigan" from *The Collected Poems of Frank O'Hara*, ©1975 by the University of California Press. Reprinted by permission of The University of California Press. GEORGE OPPEN: "Red Hook: December" from *New Collected Poems*, copy-